Awesome ALGORITHMS and Creative CODING

Clive Gifford

Crabtree Publishing Company
www.crabtreebooks.com

Crabtree Publishing Company

www.crabtreebooks.com

1-800-387-7650

Published in Canada
Crabtree Publishing
616 Welland Ave.
St. Catharines, ON
L2M 5V6

Published in the United States
Crabtree Publishing
PMB 59051, 350 Fifth Ave.
59th Floor,
New York, NY

First published in 2015 by Wayland
(A division of Hachette Children's Books)
Copyright © Wayland 2015

Author: Clive Gifford
Commissioning editor: Debbie Foy
Project Editor: Caroline West (Blue Dragonfly Ltd.)
Editorial director: Kathy Middleton
Project coordinator: Kelly Spence
Editor: Petrina Gentile
Consultant: Lee Martin, B. Ed
Designer: Mark Latter (Blue Dragonfly Ltd.)
Proofreader: Shannon Welbourn
Prepress technician: Margaret Amy Salter
Print and production coordinator: Margaret Amy Salter

Printed in Canada/022015/MA20150101

Photographs:
All images courtesy of Shutterstock except: p5
(top left) Daily Herald Archive/National
Media Museum/Science & Society Picture
Library; p5 (bottom right) Science Museum/
Science & Society Picture Library; p12 (bottom
left) Wikimedia Commons/Valiant
Technology Ltd.; p13 (top left) Valiant
Technology Ltd.; p14–15 Scratch (Scratch is a
project of the Lifelong Kindergarten Group at
the MIT Media Lab); p19 (top) Lightbot Inc.;
p28 (bottom right) IStockphoto/Ed Stock.

While every attempt has been made to clear
copyright, should there be any inadvertent
omission this will be rectified in future editions.

Disclaimer: The website addresses (URLs)
included in this book were valid at the time
of going to press. However, because of the
nature of the Internet, it is possible that some
addresses may have changed, or sites may have
changed or closed down since publication.
While the author and publisher regret any
inconvenience this may cause the readers, no
responsibility for any such changes can be
accepted by either the author or the publisher.
Note to reader: Words highlighted in bold
appear in the Glossary on page 30.
Answers to activities are on page 31.

Library and Archives Canada Cataloguing in Publication

Gifford, Clive, author
     Awesome algorithms and creative coding / Clive Gifford.

(Get connected to digital literacy)
Includes index.
Issued in print and electronic formats.
ISBN 978-0-7787-1508-5 (bound).--ISBN 978-0-7787-1558-0
(pbk.).--
ISBN 978-1-4271-1585-0 (pdf).--ISBN 978-1-4271-1581-2 (html)

     1. Computer programming--Juvenile literature. 2.
Computer
algorithms--Juvenile literature. I. Title.

QA76.6.G53 2015   j005.3   C2014-908279-7
                                                  C2014-908280-0

Library of Congress Cataloging-in-Publication Data

Gifford, Clive, author.
 Awesome algorithms and creative coding / Clive Gifford.
      pages cm. -- (Get connected to digital literacy)
 Includes index.
 ISBN 978-0-7787-1508-5 (reinforced library binding : alk. paper)
 -- ISBN 978-0-7787-1558-0 (pbk. : alk. paper) --
 ISBN 978-1-4271-1585-0 (electronic pdf : alk. paper) --
 ISBN 978-1-4271-1581-2 (electronic html : alk. paper)
 1. Computer programming--Juvenile literature. 2. Programming
languages (Electronic computers)--Juvenile literature. 3.
Computers--Juvenile literature. I. Title.

 QA76.52.G54 2015
 005--dc23

                                  2014047275

Contents

Coding Your World

HELP!

Computers are everywhere. Whenever you heat food in a microwave, watch an animated movie, or play with a smartphone, you are using computer technology. But all this technology won't work unless you tell it what to do.

IT'S YOUR TURN

Helping hands

Although computers may seem very powerful, they need people to lend a hand. Computers can't act on their own and always need a series of instructions to tell them what to do. These instructions are called programs. Writing programs is called **coding** and is carried out by people known as developers, or **programmers**.

With a program installed, computers' big brains can run super-smart code to do amazing things. For example, in 1997, IBM's Deep Blue computer—running a chess-playing program—beat the World Champion chess player, Garry Kasparov. Checkmate!

1 0 1 1 0 1

IBM 1410 computer in use at the Ford Motor Company in 1969.

I think there is a world market for maybe five computers.

TRUE STORY

Computers Galore Thomas Watson, who was once chairman of IBM, made this prediction in 1943 when computers were first invented. How wrong he was! There are believed to be over 2 billion computers in the world and millions more **smartphones** and tablets.

COMPUTER Hero!

The world's first computer programmer was a Victorian woman called Ada, Countess of Lovelace. Her friend Charles Babbage tried to build the first computers. In 1842, Ada wrote a series of instructions to do some complicated calculations on Babbage's machines, however, they were never completed. Ada had written the first computer program!

Ada, Countess of Lovelace

Algorithms in Action

All computer programs rely on algorithms. These are sets of step-by-step instructions to perform tasks or solve problems. Coders use algorithms to help them plan out their programs.

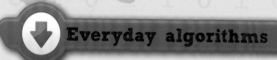 **Everyday algorithms**

You use **algorithms** all the time, probably without even knowing it. Recipes for making different foods and drinks are types of algorithms. For example, when you make a pitcher of frozen juice you have to remove the can's lid, pour the contents into a pitcher, add water, and stir. The algorithm for this task might be written as:

 1. Remove lid from frozen juice
 2. Dump juice into pitcher
 3. Turn on tap
 4. Fill pitcher with water
 5. When 3/4 full, turn off tap
 6. Stir

 Share the pretzels!

You also use algorithms to solve problems. Say you've been given a big bag of pretzels, but have to share them equally. You need to find a way to divide the pretzels out. Here are two algorithms for doing this:

Pretzel Sharing: Algorithm 1
1. Arrange everyone in a circle
2. Hand out one pretzel at a time to each person
3. When everyone has a pretzel, give yourself one
4. Repeat steps 2–3 until all the pretzels are gone

Pretzel Sharing: Algorithm 2
1. Count all the pretzels
2. Count how many people there are
3. Divide the number of pretzels by the number of people
4. Give each person the same number of pretzels as the answer

Different methods, same target

Just like the pretzel-sharing algorithms, there are many computer algorithms that can do the same job. Programmers spend a lot of time thinking through their algorithms, trying to come up with the fastest or most efficient way to perform a task.

Here are two different algorithms to tell a robot how to build a brick wall. Which algorithm do you think will get the wall built more quickly?

Robot Bricklayer: Algorithm 1
1. Go to bricks and pick up one
2. Return to wall
3. Place brick on wall
4. Repeat steps 1–3 until no bricks left

Robot Bricklayer: Algorithm 2
1. Push wheelbarrow to bricks
2. Fill wheelbarrow with all the bricks
3. Push wheelbarrow to wall
4. Place brick on wall
5. Repeat step 4 until no bricks are left

STRETCH YOURSELF

Write Instructions for a Recipe

Can you and a friend each write an algorithm for making a meal that you both like? Create detailed steps to clearly explain how to make your recipe. Compare your results:

☞ Did your friend come up with something that you didn't think of?

☞ Can you think of another recipe method that would give you the same result, but with fewer steps or that is more efficient?

My Recipes

Zeros and Ones

All computers are packed with electrical circuits. These carry tiny pulses of electricity that act like a code, sending data as streams of just two numbers: 0 and 1.

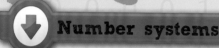

Number systems

You use the **decimal,** or base 10, number system every day when you are counting or adding. The decimal system contains 10 different digits (0, 1, 2, 3, 4, 5, 6, 7, 8, and 9). When you want to count higher than a number ending in 9, add an extra column to the left and continue counting: 10, 11, 12, and so on.

Binary is another number system. It uses only two numbers (0 and 1). Each column is worth 2 times the column to its right. The first column on the right is worth 1, the second column is 2x1=2, the third column is 2X2=4, and so on. You build a number in binary by placing a 0 or a 1 under each column. A 1 indicates you want to add that column's number to your total. A 0 means don't add that column's number in. Below is a table showing what numbers up to 15 look like in binary.

DECIMAL	0	1	2	3	4	5	6	7	8	9	10	11	12	13	14	15
BINARY	0	1	10	11	100	101	110	111	1000	1001	1010	1011	1100	1101	1110	1111

STRETCH YOURSELF

16 **17** **21**

Change Decimal to Binary

Look at the method on page 9, then see if you can work out what these three decimal numbers (right) are in binary.

Draw five columns on a piece of paper to help you.
Which numbers do you need to make the decimal number?
We've done number 15 as an example.

Column Value				
16	8	4	2	1
	1	1	1	1	=15

So, binary number 1111 is decimal number 15.

Remember you can use each number only once!

Answers on page 31

Column calculations

Binary can be turned into decimal numbers, and vice versa. You just need to remember that each column of a binary number is worth twice as much as the previous column. So, the first five columns of binary numbers equal 1, 2, 4, 8, and 16, if they are written as decimal numbers. The first column is always on the right, and you add new ones on the left.

If you write a binary number underneath the columns of decimal values, you can work out the value of the binary number. All you need to do is add together the decimal numbers that have a 1 beneath them.

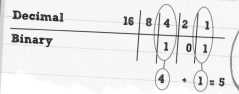

Have a look at these examples:

Convert binary number 101 to a decimal number:

Columns

	16	8	4	2	1
Decimal					
Binary			1	0	1

4 + 1 = 5

HELPFUL TIP: The binary numbers show which decimal values to add together!

Add together the decimal numbers that have a 1 beneath them.

So, binary number 1 0 1 equals decimal number 5

Convert binary number 1 0 0 1 0 to a decimal number:

Columns

	16	8	4	2	1
Decimal					
Binary	1	0	0	1	0

16 + 2 = 18

Add together the decimal numbers that have a 1 beneath them.

So, binary number 1 0 0 1 0 equals decimal number 18

STRETCH YOURSELF

Become a Binary Spy!

Make a secret number system on your left hand by using a washable marker to write 1 on your little finger, 2, 4, and 8 on your other fingers and, finally, 16 on your thumb.

You now have a binary code machine. Any finger or thumb sticking up equals a binary 1. Without speaking, can you tell a friend what number you are thinking of just by using your hand?

Here are some examples:

 Close your fist up = 0

 Give just a thumbs-up = 16

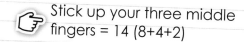 Stick up your three middle fingers = 14 (8+4+2)

Now, it's your turn... Which fingers do you need to hold up to make 6, 10, 13, and 20?

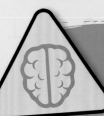

Answers on page 31

Coding Made Easier

Early computers were programmed using long series of binary numbers. These took ages to key in and also to check if a mistake was made. The invention of the compiler allowed programming languages to be created, which made coding easier.

Computer talk

A programming language is made up of commands or instructions that are like building blocks. Coders arrange these blocks in different ways to build code and programs. The language takes care of tiny but important details such as how to add up two numbers or where to store data. Some well-known computer languages are described on the next page.

BASIC

Your parents probably used this when computers first entered homes in the 1970s and 1980s. BASIC (Beginner's All-purpose Symbolic Instruction Code) used English language commands, with each command placed on a numbered line. For example, the program below will display rows of "Hello Mom" messages on a computer screen:

Hello Mom
Hello Mom
Hello Mom
Hello Mom

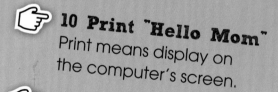 **10 Print "Hello Mom"**
Print means display on the computer's screen.

20 GOTO 10
GOTO is a BASIC command to jump to a different line number.

JAVA

This is used to write small games and programs for smartphones, tablets, and computers. Java is also used for making animated cartoons on web pages.

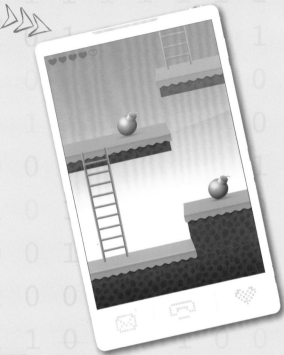

SQL

This language was developed by IBM and is used to create **databases**. A database is an application that stores large amounts of information in an organized way, so that you can find it again easily.

C++

This advanced and very powerful language has been used to write many famous computer programs. These include Microsoft Office and **browser** programs such as Google Chrome and Apple Safari that are used for viewing web pages.

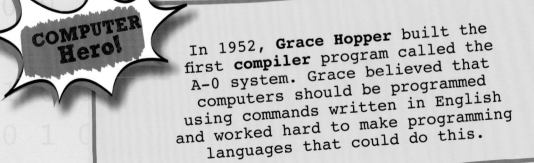

COMPUTER Hero!

In 1952, **Grace Hopper** built the first **compiler** program called the A-0 system. Grace believed that computers should be programmed using commands written in English and worked hard to make programming languages that could do this.

Languages for Learning

Every programming language has its own commands and ways of doing things. Some languages aren't that difficult and are designed for people to learn coding... including you!

STRETCH YOURSELF

Speaking LOGO!

The LOGO language was invented by an American scientist called Seymour Papert in 1967. It let children program a little robot called a turtle to move around the floor. Typing a command such as Forward 20 steps would make the robot move forward 20 steps; while typing Left 180 degrees would make it turn around 180 degrees or half a circle. Some turtle robots carried a pen so you could program them to draw on paper.

Control the Turtle

The LOGO language uses simple commands to make the turtle draw different shapes. Try using LOGO to work out the answers to these questions:

 Which one of the following shapes would this LOGO program draw?

Forward 100 steps
Left 120 degrees
Forward 100 steps
Left 120 degrees
Forward 100 steps

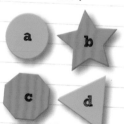

 This LOGO program makes the turtle draw a rectangle. Can you alter the first and fifth lines to make it draw a square instead?

```
Forward 120 steps
Right 90 degrees
Forward 100 steps
Right 90 degrees
Forward 120 steps
Right 90 degrees
Forward 100 steps
```

Answers on page 31

The robots are coming!

Many schools have mobile robots such as Roamers or Bee-Bots that you can program to move. You press buttons on top of the robot to enter a series of commands. These commands form a simple program. When you press "Run" or "Go," the robot carries out the commands you entered in their exact order.

Other fun languages

Other programming languages include Kodu, Python, and Scratch (see pages 14–15). Kodu uses pictures as programming commands to make fun cartoons and simple games on some personal computers and the Xbox 360 games console. Python is a text-based programming language that uses familiar-sounding words. Although Python can take longer to learn, you can use it to write many types of program.

You can program this fun Lego Mindstorms robot to move around.

STRETCH YOURSELF

Robot Rocket Launch Challenge

This set of commands describes the first eight movements the robot has to make to follow a path to his rocket. Can you work out the remaining nine commands he must follow to reach his rocket?

1. Move forward 1 space
2. Turn to the right
3. Move forward 1 space
4. Turn to the left
5. Move forward 1 space
6. Turn to the left
7. Move forward 2 spaces
8. Turn to the left

Answers on page 31

Scratch!

Scratch is one of the most popular learning languages used in schools. Scratch lets you mix sounds and pictures to create fun games and animated cartoons.

Sprite right

Scratch programs are called scripts. They feature pictures of little characters called sprites. You can program a sprite to move, change its appearance, say little messages in speech bubbles, or do something when they touch things or come across other sprites.

The first sprite you'll see in this language is a cat called Scratch. Other sprites include dinosaurs, bears, and ghosts, or you can draw your own.

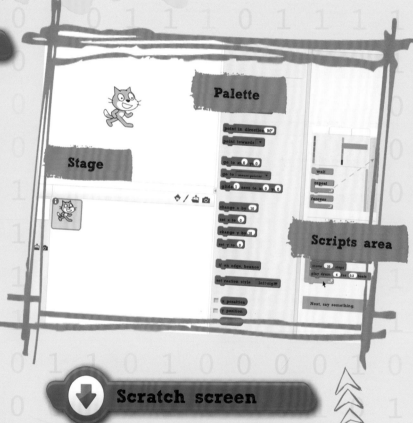

Palette

Stage

Scripts area

Scratch the Cat

Scratch screen

A Scratch screen has three main parts: the palette, scripts area, and stage. The palette stores all the Scratch instructions, called blocks, that you can use. You can pick and move the blocks from the palette to the scripts area, where you snap the blocks together to build a script to create your program. Your Scratch program is then displayed on the stage.

Scratch blocks

Many types of blocks are used in Scratch. These are all color-coded. You snap together the different blocks to build a program. Below are the ones you'll probably use the most:

MOVE 10 STEPS

Motion
Blocks like these make the sprites move across the stage and change direction.

PLAY SOUND MEOW ▼

Sounds
These blocks play sounds. You can pick a sound, such as a drum or cat's meow, or record and add your own.

WAIT 3 SECS

Events
These blocks control when parts of the script run, such as repeating some of the script or waiting a few seconds first.

SAY HELLO FOR 2 SECS

Looks
These blocks show different things such as a speech bubble or a change of costume for your sprite on the screen.

STRETCH YOURSELF

Explore Scratch!
Look at this Scratch program of a DJ cat mixing sounds. You can add to these sounds by pressing some of the keys on your keyboard. Just type this address into a web browser:

 tinyurl.com/watchdjcat

Check out other people's Scratch programs by typing this address into a web browser:

 tinyurl.com/starter-projects

Click on each screen to load the program and then on the green flag to start. You can find out what blocks were used to make each program by clicking on See Inside.

15

Accurate Algorithms

Computers need more precise instructions than you. A computer will only do what it is told and needs to be instructed very carefully. This can take lots and lots of steps.

 Be precise

People have to be very accurate when creating algorithms. Skipping over important steps or getting one wrong can mean the program doesn't work. For example, an algorithm for a robot to walk forward needs to contain steps that tell the robot to stop if it reaches a cliff edge. Otherwise, it will continue walking and fall off!

Here is another example of an algorithm, for brushing your teeth:

1. Turn on tap
2. Squeeze toothpaste onto brush
3. Use brush to clean teeth
4. Put cap on toothpaste

The algorithm doesn't say what sort of brush to use, to take the cap off the tube before squeezing it, or to turn off the tap. Oops! What steps could you add to make this algorithm work better?

TRUE STORY

$1 Million Lost In 2010, a new computer program to buy oil for an American company was switched on. But the algorithm had no limit on how many orders it could make—and so it made thousands. Experts think the company lost over $1 million in less than five seconds!

STRETCH YOURSELF

A-Maze-ing Algorithms

Build a maze with boxes and cushions. Write an algorithm of the step-by-step movements you would have to make to travel through the maze without bumping into any of the obstacles.

Blindfold a friend or parent and read out the commands in order and one at a time. They have to do exactly what you command.

Now, ask yourself these questions:

☞ Did your algorithm work the first time or did you have to make any changes?

☞ Do you need to add extra steps and commands to your algorithm?

☞ How many times did you need to try before it worked perfectly?

An answer for everything

Programmers have to think through every possibility in their algorithm. This includes what they would like to happen, but also all the things that could happen. For example, a quiz game algorithm may only need "yes" or "no" answers. But if the user types in a different word, the algorithm would have to say that it only accepts "yes" or "no" answers and ask the question again.

Breaking things down

Many tasks are made up of much smaller ones. A good algorithm breaks a task down into as small a series of steps as possible. This is called **decomposing**. For example, you could break down an algorithm for making breakfast into smaller tasks such as make toast, pour a glass of juice, and boil an egg. Each of these can then be broken down into smaller steps.

Get in Step

The steps in an algorithm have to be not only precise, but also in the right order. If you get the steps in the wrong order, then the algorithm is unlikely to work properly.

Jumping around

Keeping track of the steps in an algorithm can become more complicated if it is designed to jump back to an earlier point. This simple algorithm on the right keeps track of a soccer player taking shots on goal. But the score isn't going up each time he scores. Can you work out what is wrong with the algorithm?

1. Score = 0
2. Player shoots
3. Was a goal scored?
4. If a goal wasn't scored, go to line 2
5. If a goal was scored, add one to Score and go to line 1

This algorithm almost works, but every time line 5 adds one to the score, it jumps back to line 1, which sets the score to zero again! The solution is simple: line 5 should end with "go to line 2."

STRETCH YOURSELF

Can You Fix the Algorithm?
Here are some instructions for having a bath, but they're all jumbled up. Can you put them in the right order?

1. Put in bath plug
2. Get dressed
3. Fill bath with water
4. Get into the bath
5. Wash
6. Take out bath plug
7. Get out of the bath
8. Get undressed

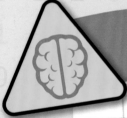

Answers on page 31

18

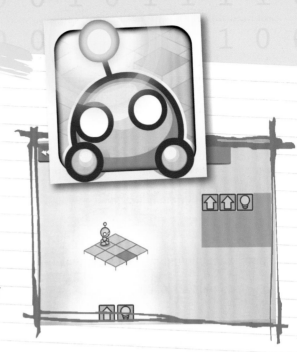

Make Lightbot Move!

If you have Internet access, why not visit and play with Lightbot? This fun game lets you choose from a series of simple commands to build a program that will make the little robot move.

The tasks start off easy, but get harder, so you really have to think through what commands to use and in what order.

You can visit Lightbot by typing this address into a web browser: **tinyurl.com/light-robot-game**

 ## Subroutines

Some parts of an algorithm, such as displaying a message on screen, may be needed again and again. But this means that the algorithm can get very long. So, smart coders write these parts as sections called **subroutines.**

Developers only have to write a subroutine once and then direct the program to jump to it when it needs to use it. This makes writing complicated programs easier and faster.

HIGH SCORE
768.987.000

In this game, when a player shoots a spider, the program goes to a subroutine to show an explosion and then another subroutine to add points to the score displayed on screen.

Decisions, Decisions

Most computer programs have to make decisions along the way. Although some decisions are simple, more complicated ones need to be broken down into lots of small decisions.

 If... Then...

Many programs ask a computer to make decisions based on the information that they receive using an IF statement. This states that IF something is true, THEN the program will respond and do something.

In computer programs, decisions are made all the time. For example, in the car-racing game below, the game's code has to make lots of different decisions. Then, when the program for the race decides that the game should end, it runs a particular piece of code to give the player a final score and prints "Game Over" on the computer screen. This is called **code selection**.

If the player presses the accelerator, then speed up the car

If the car bumps into another car, then slow down the car and make a crashing sound

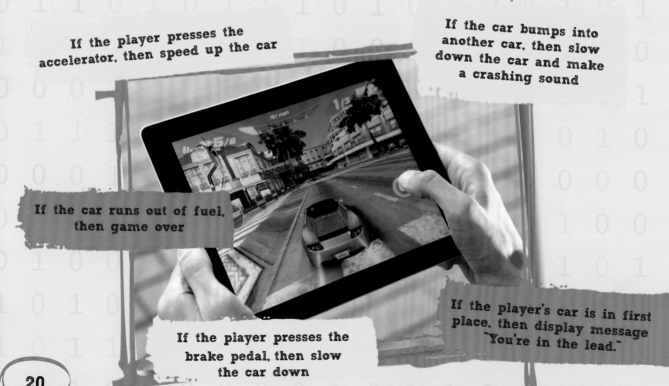

If the car runs out of fuel, then game over

If the player presses the brake pedal, then slow the car down

If the player's car is in first place, then display message "You're in the lead."

Some decisions are made in programs using different symbols to compare data. These include the greater than **>** and lesser than **<** symbols, which are used to compare numbers. For example, a program to grade the results out of 10 in a child's spelling test might look like this:

Spelling Test Code

If spelling test score ≤4, then print "Try Again!" and End Program

If spelling test score ≥8, then print "Excellent!" and End Program

Print "Good, But Keep Trying!" and End Program

Challenge:
Which scores out of 10 would earn the "Good, But Keep Trying" mark in the above code and which would earn an "Excellent?"

Answers on page 31

Lists of objects or numbers can be sorted out by making decisions. For example, a program might compare different numbers to work out which are bigger and which are smaller.

A series of decisions can be shown in a branching tree diagram. The one below shows the decisions an algorithm could make when sorting out a list of objects.

Is it a toy?

Yes   No

Does it have legs?   Does it have a handle?

No   Yes   No   Yes

It's a ball   It's a bear   It's a pillow   It's a mug

21

Go with the Flow

Programmers need to think through all the possible things that can happen in an algorithm or program and check that all the parts work in the right way and in the right order.

Follow the flow chart

Many programmers use a diagram called a **flow chart** to map out their algorithm or program. This helps them to find errors and make improvements.

A flow chart can contain four different shapes or symbols, including an oval, rectangle, diamond, and **parallelogram**. These are connected by arrows to show the different stages and flow of information in a program. Each shape or symbol means a different thing.

Flow Chart Symbols

Terminator

Oval shapes show the start or end of a whole program, or just part of a program.

Process

Rectangular shapes show that something happens, such as numbers being added together.

Decision

Diamond shapes show where a program makes a decision. This is usually a simple decision such as "yes" or "no," or "true" or "false."

PLEASE ENTER YOUR NAME

Input/Output

Parallelogram shapes either mean that the program accepts an **input,** like the click of a computer mouse, or **outputs** data, such as displaying a message or picture on screen.

22

Flow charts in action

Here is a simple flow chart to show an algorithm for how a player makes a move in a game of Snakes and Ladders.

STRETCH YOURSELF

Fix the Flow Chart
This flow chart shows an algorithm for working out why a lamp isn't working. There are some gaps in the flow chart. Can you work out which pieces of circled text go in each gap?

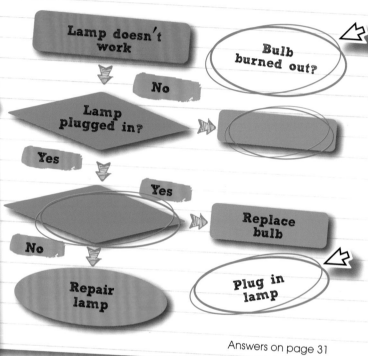

Answers on page 31

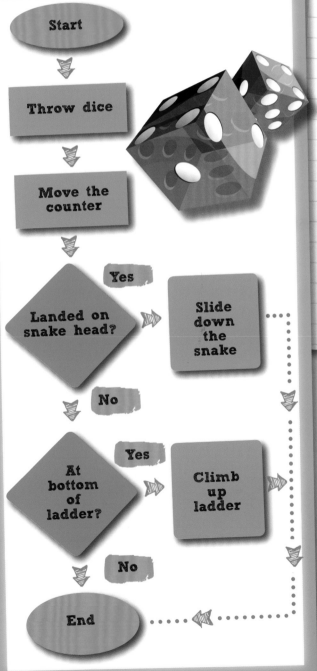

COMPUTER Hero!

Frank Bunker Gilbreth was an engineer who enjoyed making jobs as simple as possible. In 1921, Frank introduced the first flow charts to map out workers' jobs. Flow charts would later become popular with computer programmers.

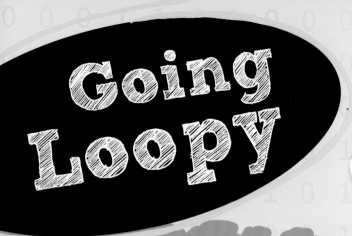

Going Loopy

The instructions in a loop will happen again and again as long as the loop continues.

Computers are good at performing the same task over and over again without making any mistakes. Lots of computer programs take advantage of this to get jobs done.

Loops and variables

The repeating parts of a program are called **loops**. These often use little stores of data called **variables**. A variable's value can alter and be used to count things in a program.

Computers use variables in a program to remember things such as a player's score in a game. A variable is given a name and is a sort of box that can hold information such as a number or a series of letters. This is known as a **string**. So, a variable to store your age might be age=9 and another could be name=James. Variables can be changed by code in the program.

Count on us

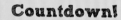

Loops are useful for counting events or things, especially when they are used with variables that keep track of how many times something has happened.

The loop below counts down the seconds until a rocket lifts off. Each time the program goes through the loop, the value of the variable seconds goes down by one. The loop ends on lift-off, which is when the variable seconds equals zero.

```
Countdown!
Seconds = 60
Repeat
    Seconds = Seconds -1
    Show on screen: Seconds
    Until Seconds = 0
```

In a loop

Some loops continue for as long as the program runs. These are called infinity loops. Other loops, like the countdown loop on page 24, are told to repeat a set number of times.

Conditional loops are another type of loop. They keep repeating the steps in the loop until something else happens. For example, this algorithm for a store checkout scanner might allow only 10 items or fewer to be scanned. If more are attempted, then the scanning loop ends.

Ten Items Or Fewer

N = 0

N is a variable. It equals the number of items scanned. It is set to zero to start with because nothing has been scanned.

Loop
Scan item
For each item scanned, let N = N+1

One is added to the number of items scanned.

If N > 10, ring bell and display "No more than 10 items!"
and Leave Loop
Loop Again

STRETCH YOURSELF

Fix the Time

Here is a loop that is part of a digital clock program. It's not working properly because it shows the time 02:07 as 01:67. Can you work out which of the three numbered lines below should replace the circled line to get the program working properly?

Minutes = 0

Minutes is the name of a variable.

Hours = 0

Hours is also a variable.

Loop

Minutes = Minutes +1

<u>If Minutes = 60, Then Hours = Hours+1</u>

If Hours = 24, Then Hours = 0

 1. If Minutes = 60, Then end loop

 2. If Minutes = 60, Then Minutes = 0 and Hours = Hours+1

 3. If Minutes = 67, Then Minutes = Hours

Answers on page 31

01:67

02:07

A Bug's Life

Only some programs work the very first time. Programmers expect errors to happen. These errors are known as bugs. Getting rid of bugs in a program is called debugging.

 Check and test

Some programming errors are just typing mistakes such as keying in the wrong number or misspelling a command. These are often spotted by carefully checking all the program code. Other errors, though, are more complicated and may take a long time to solve.

Programmers often break their program down into small parts and then run and test each part to try and find the problem.

Testing times

Testing takes place throughout the time a computer program is being developed. Sometimes, computer users are asked to test out the programs. They act as **beta testers** and report back any bugs or problems that they find.

ERROR

Launch failure

Some bugs in programs can be devastating. A bug in the guidance computer of an Ariane 5 space rocket made the rocket veer off target and finally self-destruct just a minute after lift-off in 1996.

TRUE STORY

Moths In 1947, a dead moth caused a switch to malfunction inside the Harvard Mark II, one of the first computers. The programmers stuck the moth into the computer's logbook. It was computing's first "bug!"

Catch the Bug

This flow chart shows the parts of a program for playing tag. But one of the arrows is in the wrong place for the program to work properly.

Can you work out which arrow is wrong, and where it should go?

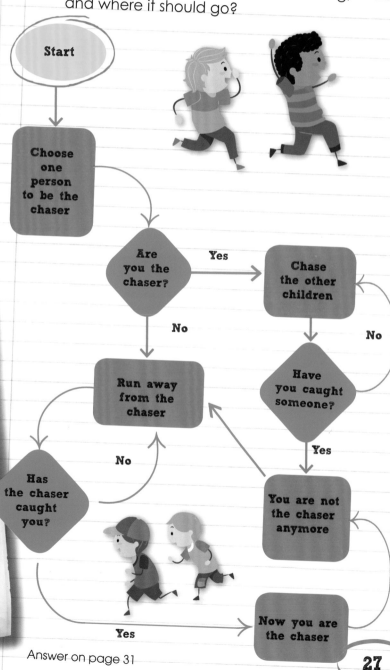

Start

Choose one person to be the chaser

Are you the chaser? — Yes → Chase the other children

No

Run away from the chaser

Have you caught someone? — No

Yes

You are not the chaser anymore

Has the chaser caught you?

No

Yes

Now you are the chaser

Answer on page 31

Coding Careers

Think you might become a whiz at computer coding when you get older? If so, then there may be some great jobs for you when you grow up.

⬇ Working together

In the past, computer programs and code were often written by only one person. Today, many major applications and games need dozens or even hundreds of people to build them.

Some people work out what the program should do, while others write and test the code. Many other coders work on existing programs, writing code for new features, or debugging problems with the latest program.

COMPUTER Hero!

Jack Dorsey was fascinated by coding as a child. In 2006, Dorsey and his business partner, Biz Stone, wrote the first version of the Twitter social networking app in just two weeks. Over 500 million "tweets" are now sent every day.

Jack Dorsey

Think big

The programs you use on a computer are often huge projects. A typical iPhone app may have 30,000 lines of code, while a complex computer game can have over a million! Even bigger is the Windows 8 operating system, which contains about 40 million lines of code. Phew!

Young coders – just like you!

Computer coding can be a job for life. For example, Markus "Notch" Persson was a programming whiz-kid. He wrote his first computer game using BASIC when he was an 8-year-old boy! When he grew up, Markus wrote games for Jalbum. He left his job to create his own hit game: Minecraft.

TRUE STORY

World Wide Fun The game Tetris was created in 1984 by a computer engineer named Alexey Pajitnova. Tetris has since been reprogrammed to work on lots of computers, phones, and tablets.

STRETCH YOURSELF

Write a Computer Program

Can you think of a computer program that would make your life easier?

Try to sketch out all of its different parts.

Then, ask yourself these questions:

 How would the program operate?

 What would the program need to know?

 What controls would users need to use it?

 What problems can you see in advance?

Glossary

algorithm A set of steps that are followed in order to solve a problem or perform a task

beta tester A person who tests a computer program that is almost finished to try and find any bugs or problems

binary Also known as base 2, binary is a number system that contains just two digits: 1 and 0

browser A type of computer program used by people to view websites on the World Wide Web

code selection When a program is told to run a particular piece of code after making a decision, such as running the code that says "Game Over" and giving a final score when the program decides the game has ended

coding Writing the lines of code in a program that make a computer or other device work

compiler A computer program that converts instructions written in a programming language into code that a computer can understand and act on

database A program that allows people to store huge amounts of information on computers with ease

decimal Also known as base 10, decimal is the number system that you use every day. It contains the digits, 0, 1, 2, 3, 4, 5, 6, 7, 8, and 9

decomposing Breaking down a complicated task into smaller parts or steps, making it easier to understand and write code

debugging To identify and remove errors in a computer program

flow chart A type of diagram that maps out the actions and decisions that occur within a program or part of a program

input Data or commands that a user enters into a computer using a keyboard or by pressing a touch screen on a tablet

loop A part of a computer program that repeats the same steps and instructions over and over again. Many loops are conditional—they continue until a condition is met or an order instructs them to stop

output The results of a computer's processing and work. Output is often displayed on a screen

parallelogram A shape with opposite sides that are parallel and also equal in length

programmer A person who writes computer code and programs, either for fun or as a job

smartphone Powerful mobile phone that contains a mini computer which allows users to view videos, listen to music, and run lots of different programs

string A type of variable (see below) that stores one or more letters or other characters

subroutine A section of a program which performs a task and can be jumped back to as many times as the whole program needs

variable A location for storing information in a program which can be changed by other parts of the program

30

Further Resources

Books

Understanding Programming and Logic
by Matthew Anniss
(Heinemann Raintree, 2015)

Quick Expert's Guide: Computing and Programming
by Shahneila Saeed (Wayland, 2015)

Quick Expert's Guide: Creating an App
by Chris Martin (Wayland, 2014)

How Things Work: Electrical Gadgets
by Ade Deane-Pratt
(PowerKids Press, 2011)

Websites

www.commonsensemedia.org/lists/coding-apps-and-websites
A great page containing links to lots of different computer activities and languages to help you learn about coding.

www.helpkidscode.com
A website for parents, teachers, and older children.

http://learn.code.org/hoc/1
A video tutorial which helps you use the Blockly coding language to create a simple program.

www.light-bot.com/hocflash.html
Have fun programming an on-screen robot called Lightbot.

www.scratch.mit.edu
Learn more about coding by creating programs starring Scratch the Cat and other fun characters.

www.wordfreegames.com/game/binary-game.html
A groovy game to help teach you how to use binary numbers.

Answers

page 8
Change Decimal to Binary:
16 = 10000
17 = 10001
21 = 10101

page 9
Become a Binary Spy!:
6 = Your middle and fourth finger
10 = Your index and fourth finger
13 = Your index, middle, and little finger
20 = Your thumb and middle finger

page 12
Control the Turtle:
* The LOGO program would draw the equilateral triangle (answer d)

* The first and fifth lines should both say "Forward 100 steps."

page 13
Robot Rocket Launch Challenge:
Here are the rest of the commands the robot will need in order to reach his rocket.

9. Move forward 1 space
10. Turn to the right
11. Move forward 1 space
12. Turn to the right
13. Move forward 2 spaces
14. Turn to the right
15. Move forward 4 spaces
16. Turn to the left
17. Move forward 1 space

page 18
Can You Fix the Instructions?:
1. Put in bath plug
3. Fill bath with water
8. Get undressed
4. Get into the bath
5. Wash
7. Get out of the bath
6. Take out bath plug
2. Get dressed

page 21
Spelling Test Code Challenge:
* The scores 4, 5, 6, 7, and 8 would earn a "Good, But Keep Trying" mark.

* The scores 9 and 10 would earn an "Excellent!" mark.

page 23
Fix the Flow Chart:
* "Plug in lamp" should go in the blue rectangular shape.

* "Bulb burned out?" should go in the green diamond shape.

page 25
Fix the Time:
Line number 2 should replace the circled line.

page 27
Catch the Bug:
The arrow at the bottom right of the chart is in the wrong place. To debug the program, this arrow should point from "Now you are the chaser" to "Chase the other children."

Index